SURVIVING SELF-PUBLISHING

or

Why Ernest Hemingway Committed Suicide

AVA GREENE

ISBN 978-1-938691-13-3

At least 30% of the proceeds from "Surviving Self-Publishing"
goes to protecting wilderness, wildlife, and all creatures of land
and sea from human violation, insensitivity, and ignorance.

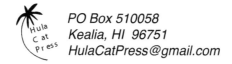

PO Box 510058
Kealia, HI 96751
HulaCatPress@gmail.com

This book is respectfully dedicated

to everyone who's given their all,

found their quest way harder than they dreamed,

and stayed the course.

TABLE OF CONTENTS

ACKNOWLEDGEMENTS

Nowhere does the word 'self' have the depth of meaning it does in 'self-publishing.' Well, maybe in sailing solo from California to Japan on a raft of logs. Or maybe in that song, "You Picked a Fine Time to Leave Me, Lucille." For authors, this four-letter s-word seems to accumulate onerous implication like a snowball picking up powder on a steep downhill roll.

Because of the scope of self-publishing and the isolation in which it's undertaken, we're all indebted to those who've both published before us and left blogs for us to follow. Reading their guidance, any writer with a book or book idea can not only study every aspect of self-publishing, but actually publish books alone! Every step of the way, s/he can find free and valuable direction, advice, tutorials, support, plus all levels of paid help. And there's friendliness, generosity, reverence for the written word, and a love of books that permeate this on-line industry still in its infancy.

It takes guts to toss one's hat into the ring of indie book marketing. But on line, each newcomer is warmly welcomed by writers of every age and genre, all of whom relate to your dream and are empathically aware how you spend your hours. The pen, ink, keyboard, and Internet bind writers together now into a sharing community that never before existed. Despite an author's physical solitude, there's instant access to answers, information, inspiration, and even sympathy any time of the day or night.

So, I gratefully acknowledge the leaders and contributors of the on-line self-publishing universe. It's they who make publishing possible for all of us! Without listing the many names, I assure all readers of THIS book that, should you go on to publish, or continue to publish, you'll come to know and appreciate bloggers of every stripe who passionately offer up their experience. Here's to those who light the way!

And, hey, a fringe benefit to this venture is that everything we read while progressing the course is well written!

XOXOXOXOX

INTRO / DISCLAIMER

In this book, I'm sharing *my* approaches (so far) to self-publishing and selling books a) without hiring book designers, b) without hiring PR professionals, c) without spending much, and d) without becoming a publicity wizard. But this is not a how-to guide for getting manuscripts into books, it's not a writing instructional, and not a road-map to bestseller status. This is a survival manual—I'm addressing the side of the business nobody likes to talk about.

I started out with no technical prowess, no financial backing, no supportive spouse/lover/parent, and no already-self-published friend/relation/ acquaintance to look to for guidance. I just saw that self-publishing was possible, I lacked the fortitude for endlessly querying traditional publishers with poor odds of acceptance, and I believed my books deserved readers. Self-publishing was my only option, and perhaps an opportunity.

So I started research and development in 2011 and published my first book, "Some Swamis are Fat," in 2012.

But the big question about self-publishing seems to remain unanswered: Does it actually work that well for the vast majority of self-made authors? Judging by the lion's share of internet commentary, most are still trying to crack the code....

In these pages, you'll get insight and fair warning about what to expect and how to prepare. For the amount of time, emotion, and hard labor that go into writing a book, it's mandatory to have good intel about the terrain ahead.

Aspiring authors of any genre will benefit from this text, but the book's somewhat geared toward creative writers, those writing from passion and love of craft, rather than those teaching how to tune pianos or profiling the best hikes in San Diego County. Obviously everyone's deeply involved in any book they've written, but those dreaming of published novels or memoirs probably have more unrealistic perceptions about what self-publishing might deliver and what it entails.

I'll also add that the fewer books you've already self-published — none being just as valid as one or several — the more these chapters will bolster you. If you've already produced numerous books, your journey has some definition and momentum by now and won't necessarily parallel mine. But whatever sort of writer you are, know that this isn't meant to accelerate hopes about what's ahead for 'anyone who really wants it.' This isn't Rocky III—how to beat the odds and become America's next little darling—it's a *survival* manual.

I'm by no means saying *avoid* self-publishing, but not everyone should attempt it. From *your* unique writer perspective and from whence you've cometh, you must weigh your own stamina and willingness against realistic estimations of the workload and payload ahead. If you're serious about publishing, you need this data!

So…one reviewer of this book said I seem a bit angry and the book should be happier. To clarify, I'm not angry, but neither am I fake. Maybe I'm too frank. But isn't it better to come out the other side in one piece with something to show for it? Isn't it best to stay willing to keep growing and learning? And to work with sound expectations so you can proceed strategically? 'Angry' isn't the right word—because I've mastered an amazing skill, I have beautiful published books, and I continue to sell them and receive five-star reviews. But 'publisher's fatigue' might be a malady I've contracted a time or two, a weak or deflated state of mind suggesting the writer take a little breather in the shade.

Moving right along, this is really more an open letter to interested parties than what I'd call a real book. In my 'real' books, I labor endlessly over every component of writing and publishing because I'm making a permanent contribution to the literary world. This is shot from the hip—something I'm compelled to offer, despite the shifting sands of this business. But if I continue tweaking it indefinitely, as the industry evolves, I'll be writing forever and it won't see the light of day. So I hope you find the contents timely and useful to whatever phase of self-publishing you're in or striving for. Grab what you can, and cut me some slack for not re-writing it twenty more times. Namaste.

As a final note, this book is not front-loaded, so read all the way through to get all the nuggets and tidbits. Then write a review!

XOXOXOX

– 1 –

HELLO

Welcome to self-publishing. If you're reading this, it's a clear indicator you've got one or more books burning inside. I feel you. I've been there. I'm still there.

For me, the three main mantras are quality, being true to myself, and staying willing. But your trip is up to you. Perhaps, like me, you're a die-hard who identifies with your story, your writing, your stamina and drive. If you are said pioneer, if you like figuring things out and learning, if you like full control over the process, then take this info to heart and know you're not alone. Ultimately, you'll have published books with your name on them and YOU made it happen.

As stated, you won't be given step-by-step instructions and pointers here, or compendiums of resources about how to self-publish. All that's accessible on line (in exchange for a few years of your time). And there are far too many idiosyncrasies of each writer and each book to be dealt with in a treatment like this book. My aim is to soften some of the inevitable frustration by tipping you off about what to expect. You'll read about surprises and trials you'll inevitably encounter, ups and downs, and what can make it all worthwhile. I may shatter some illusions, but perhaps, like me, you prefer non-fiction when it comes to the whys and wherefores of taking on something this big.

I'll say one thing with certainty: If you read this whole book, take it seriously, and continue on to publish, you'll thank me for the heads-up. You might even refer back here later, nodding (or shaking) your head and chuckling (or weeping) at my brutal honesty. I guarantee this book will toughen you up.

Finally — and I don't get into this deeply in the book, but — self-publishing, for all its torturous detail, is entirely do-able. Few authors publish numerous paperbacks (and ebooks) all by their lonesome, with perhaps one or two professional edits per book. Few have the fortitude, wherewithal, or even desire to become a full-on publisher as well as an author of multiple titles. I am such a person — with four published paperbacks and ebooks (five, counting this one), two more in the works, and even a compact home studio ready now to produce audio books. I've learned the full whammy of getting books from manuscript to someone's book shelf and that's why I know you can do it.

So, isn't it reassuring to know you CAN write and produce charming books with complete professionalism? You can!

Fyi, this book is published under a pen name. So if you look for the other books I claim to have written, they're not under Ava Greene. On the last page of this book, you'll find my books listed, along with my other author name. And, of course, they're on Amazon, where you can read the reviews. (One of my books, 'Some Swamis are Fat,' is published under Ava Greene.)

XOXOXOX

- 2 -

SHOULD I SELF-PUBLISH ?

Let's acknowledge the hyena in the room: Why not query traditional publishers? "I think Random House or Penguin wants me…. No? They don't? But I'm a great writer with a modern classic! Three years hence, it will be a movie. Of course they want me, I just have to get their attention!"

Okay, go ahead and spend years collecting rejection letters. Or…save the time and query traditional publishers *while* you self-publish. In self-publishing, you can do whatever you want because you own the rights. Query forever; you might be correct and traditional publishers will jump all over your masterpiece one day. They really might, but don't burn out trying.

Personally, I lack the patience for that. And, in my observation, there are basically only four circumstances under which traditional publishers might sign you on. I do not fall into any of them, but perhaps you do:

1. You're famous. Or you can ghost-write for celebrities and ride on the coattails of this division.

2. You have a highly topical story relating to contemporary issues, like 'I Was a Juvenile Gang Leader, Now I'm Baltimore Chief of Police' or 'I'm a Monsanto Lobbyist Turned Vegan Environmentalist.' Actually, that one sounds more like a sitcom or Michael Moore documentary.

3. You have such a massive 'author platform' — a social media following of many, many thousands or more — for either yourself ('I Lost 400 Pounds') or your subject matter ('The Exotic Mating Ritual of the Laysan Albatross of the Sandwich Islands'*) that your adoring tribe will devour anything you offer.

4. You've already written one blockbuster and this is your next sure bet: 'Book 2: A Hooker's Eye-view of Mar-a-Lago's Chandeliers.' This one actually also falls under categories 1 and 2.

One-two-three-four. That's it. Traditional publishers will not take you unless it's a slam-dunk. Why? They can't. Just as you don't want to do all the hard work for no money, neither do they. Plus, they have to pay your cut as well as all the normal expenses. It's their money, they have to be prudent how they spend it.

Just say hello to self-publishing and don't look back.

Sure, it may seem more prestigious to get a traditional deal — "Yay, Penguin wants my book!" — yet this doesn't always mean they'll sell tons of books for you. Even with a flurry of sales in the beginning, there's no promise, guarantee, or even overwhelming evidence that authors sell more books through trad publishers. Yes, they'll initially market your book. Yes, your book will be in book stores. Yes, it will probably look pretty decent. And, yes, you've got a team that likely knows significant-ly more than you about publishing, so you're off the hook. The glossy, upfront part of the promotion will be commandeered by them — the launch, initial marketing, and groovy presentation. But, though you possibly sell more books, you make less per book, you sign away all the rights for usually three years or longer, it takes at least a year for your book to be published, you then have to wait another six months to a year for royalty checks, and you've got to go through your publisher to make any changes to your book. They have creative control. You have a say, but if someone else is designing your book, that's their job and they really don't want little in-experienced you breathing down their collar. Your job is to write, get back to your desk.

Also, you've got an editor assigned to you — you didn't choose that person. Hopefully the relationship is one of mutual respect and good humor, but you can't simply replace that individual if you're displeased. Ditto for the cover designer assigned to your book.

In addition, unforeseen circumstances beyond your control can sabotage even traditionally published books. What if your book had been slated for release on September 11, 2001? No one was buying books that day, that month, or that season. Or say another big book by some huge super-star is released the same day or week....

As an analogy, take Farrah Fawcett, as big a Hollywood actress in her day as anyone. Teenage boys had her poster in their bedrooms in the late 'sixties and early 'seventies. Later on, she got cancer and suffered for years. People cared and followed her story, there was even a film about all her last-ditch treatments in Europe. The weird thing was, she died the same day as Michael Jackson, who wasn't sick and whose death was a total blindside. Though Farrah Fawcett was a huge celebrity with a decades-long story of beauty, glamour, fame, fortune, and misfortune, because she passed when something mega was dominating the news, her death was practically ignored.

Bad analogy, I know, but if you traditionally publish, something similar could conceivably happen to you (well, not death) if a more prominent book or some other splash eclipses your book release.

Traditional publishing doesn't ensure more success. You'll just get a bigger, better send-off, you may get a monetary advance, you'll get a toe-hold in book stores, and they'll do the publishing part for you. But it takes a long time to a) get signed, and b) finally see your book in print. You don't learn the publishing ropes. And, should your book not perform well enough, it's doubtful they'll give you another shot. Your second book could end up self-published anyway. Might as well learn how to do it.

Or do both. 'Hybrid' authors self-publish some books and trad-publish others. You can even have two names, pen-name and real name. Some authors write in several genres — memoir over here, science-fiction over there. Here's my Cowboy Romance, there's my 'Teach Your Cat to Hula.' All good. You can approach this from any number of angles. Freedom is a major upside of self-publishing. (An unexplored facet, actually. Most self-pubbers are so busy mimicking traditional publishers, they're missing an exciting opportunity to break the mold!)

Ava Greene

* The Laysan Albatross really are amazing birds! I have a video of them on my YouTube channel. I actually live in the Sandwich Islands, a.k.a. the larger archipelago containing the Hawaiian Islands.

XOXOXOX

- 3 -

THE MYTH

The biggest myth of all—I don't know where it came from, but unpublished writers unanimously subscribe to it—is that strangers perusing Amazon.com will stumble across your book and buy it.

Take my word for it, they won't.

Ever.

With twenty trazillion books on Amazon and ten kazillion more added per year, no one is browsing around looking for some one-off book to buy and read. *No one*. Please believe me. If, by some fluke, someone is, then the chance they crash-land on your page, then actually make the purchase, is a bazillion to none. The only people who are going to find your book on Amazon are people YOU send there to check it out. And even they won't buy it unless they fall squarely into your niche market

('Whale Watching for Dummies') or they love you, want to date you, are mesmerized by your marketing panache, or you offer a discount.

Compare it to airline tickets. Would you buy a random ticket to, say, Argentina? No. Well, only if someone a) sells you on the idea, then b) helps you get a good deal on airfare. Otherwise you're taking the family to Disney World.

The only reason I embarked on this journey was because I had about ten books I wanted to publish someday. Some were written, others partially written. At a cost of maybe $10,000 per book if I hired professionals, I'd have to sell my house. Also, when I started out in 2011, I thought this would be *much* easier. And there was no book like this one to prime me for the carnival ride. Plus, after I'd convinced myself to self-publish and was neck-deep, it always seemed foolish to scrap all the time and research and throw in the towel. Four books later (now five), here I am.

But no, I'm not going to publish your book. No matter how much you offer, I'm not doing it! (Then again—how much you got? ;-))

Regarding self-publishing, if you're a one-book wonder, **don't even undergo the pains and strains to learn the process**. It's worth spending the money and hiring the talent to help you. Save your energy for the writing. Save your chutzpah for conferring with the editor of your choice. And save your emotions for marketing. Because, irregardless of whether you do everything yourself or farm all or part of it out, you still have to market the thing. (Sorry.) Even if you hire pros, you've got to find them, establish a flow with them, fathom what they're doing, monitor them, change things that aren't what you wanted, and pay them. And you're going to be a marketeer once the book is out, no matter where and how you sell it.

Right now you feel like you're a good or great writer, but hardly anyone's seen your stuff, you're out in the literary boonies. Meanwhile, there's a giant world out there of books, publishing, and authorship you want into. You may also feel, as I did, that you'd be cheating yourself to never have a published book. Okay, if you're serious about this, then, in your publisher hat, you'll travel to the other side of the writer experience. You'll learn the ins and outs of a complex trade that maybe you don't feel cut out for, but that, in the end, will leverage you and your writing.

XOXOXOX

- 4 -

SET THE STAGE

In order to really sell some books, have a decent time doing it, and come to comprehend marketing better, let's set the stage a little.

For any business venture, there are requirements for getting ready. For example, would you open a store if you didn't even have a car to ferry materials to and from that shop, and to commute to it and back? Would you order a line of products to sell if you had nowhere to store or place them? For indie authors, envisioning the end game for both you and your product(s) is a good exercise before starting. Visualize an outcome and ask yourself key questions: How do you want your author progression to play out? Where and how is it going to take place? How long might it take to get where you'd like to be? (Warning: being agonizingly realistic, you'll still be legions off the true time-line.) Think things through before setting out.

If you simply envision your three children each holding, and cherishing forever, a glistening hardback of your memoir, go ahead and print ten books (hiring any help you need), pass them around, and tell other interested parties they can order their signed copy through you. Boom, you're done.

If you just want to get your teeth wet and see if you can indeed become a bonafide author of a paperback book that can be purchased on Amazon, go ahead and do that. It's not that hard. (Again, just pay others to handle aspects you cannot manage yourself.) If you have a niche book related to a passion or your life's work—pearl-diving, Turkish rugs, alcoholism, Uncle Fester's possum pie recipes—enhance your sphere of influence and expand your expertise with a handsome book to sell at events and speaking engagements. Whip up a snappy business card, sell some books locally, and enjoy being an author. Ditto for your ebook. Boom, you're done.

Or maybe you're more ambitious. (Ambition for self-publishers isn't necessarily a good thing, once you glimpse what's ahead for you and your ego.) Let's say you want to make actual green money from your writing. Maybe you believe you're an engaging, gifted, or highly-informed writer. Maybe you've been a writer in other capacities and now want to do books. Maybe you have a few bucket-list books you need to finish and publish. Maybe you believe you're sitting on valuable data or a fabulous story there's an audience for. Or perhaps there's some horrendous truth you want to unshackle yourself from…. Each writer has his/her own motivation.

But you can't emulate anybody else's blow-by-blow game-plan, you have to craft your own. So the first task is to think things through. Try answering the following questions to define your author self. Maybe jot down your answers.

1. What is the look and feel of your completed book? Picture its size, approximate length, style of cover, the visual feel of it, and the tone it suggests to a reader. What's the genre? What's the price of the book? Can you think of other authors or other books that resonate in the way your book might?

For example, is your book scary? Is it funny? Is it shocking? Other-worldly? Hot and steamy? Prophetic? Do you have your distinct cast of characters? In what section of a book store would it be found?

2. Have you pulled out all the stops to produce the best manuscript possible? If not, make sure you do. See you next year.

3. Can you afford to hire an editor, a cover artist, and a book designer—or a company that packages these for you? (This is still self-publishing and you're still the publisher.) There are dozens and dozens of book design services and editors to choose from, and endless criteria to weigh in the choosing. If you don't consign help, you either have to do everything yourself—doable for true die-hards—or forget self-publishing. I admit to being a die-hard, but only recommend it to black-belt masochists. On the other hand, I've done better than most self-pubbers, strictly due to being a die-hard!

If you do everything yourself, you have to learn book formatting through the Adobe InDesign Creative Suites software (or Word, but I'm not sure about Word because I use InDesign), and Adobe Photoshop and/or Adobe Illustrator for covers (or Canva, for the non-pros). Again, there are surely other options, but these Adobe software programs are what professionals and die-hards use since the programs are so comprehensive. Note that you can purchase Adobe software for a small fortune or, instead, buy second-hand computers already rigged with everything you need. Since 2011, I've purchased two Mac laptops from Craigslist, that came with all the Adobe programs and have served me wondrously ever since.

4. Are you ready to set the stage for selling increasing numbers of books over a period of years, or is a one-shot deal more suitable to your lifestyle and author vision?

5. Can you conceive of the ongoing marketing process as inventive and somehow in sync with your author persona?

6. Are you able to make time for the desk work and demands of continually producing and selling books? How would this affect and impact your psyche/relationships/family/job/health/finances/pets?

7. Are you durable enough to take the hits — suggestions for improvements from editors or beta readers; having to do re-writes, re-formatting, re-working the cover dozens of times; screw-ups in the first printings of your books and covers; screw-ups on your Amazon listing (even on launch week or launch day); having your book-release date come many months or years after you calculated; people letting you down by not buying, not reading, or not reviewing your book; maybe some less-than-five-star

reviews; earnings moving at a snail's pace when you thought the pivotal moment of your life had arrived; watching your goals recede into the distance as marketing chores form rings around your brain; weathering the changes to your perceptions about how this journey would or 'should' be?

8. Are you willing to leave your comfort zone in terms of sharing your story, letting the public in, and presenting yourself physically? If not, some aspects of selling may not suit you.

9. Are you willing to embrace the Internet/ smart phone/global network/social media components of marketing? There's no other way and it gets more multi-faceted daily. If you're technologically blocked, you'll need towering stacks of cash to pay for assistance.

10. Are you excited about the boot camp ahead? Publishing a book yourself means publishing a book *yourself*; it's not a metaphor. Do you possess the patience for continuous learning, including the ever-changing technologies?

11. Can you accept that unforeseen tasks will side-swipe you on a regular basis? And that, as you reach goals, you won't be basking in the sun but squinting at the next line-up of challenges?

12. Are you able to do the recordkeeping? Do you have the vigilance to log your true costs, record eventual profits, format alien accounting procedures, keep track of all the different venues selling your books, handle tax responsibilities? Designing customized spread-sheets is a must as you develop more markets and more books.

13. Are you willing to ultimately — maybe later, possibly sooner — delegate some of the workload and relinquish some control in order to grow your business? If so, which components of the business are you willing to off-load? (I have not done this yet.)

14. Are you ready to embark on a long and soulful passage, from which you will never fully return to your current incarnation?

15. Can you — this is a nasty one — accept that the amount of money you'll make in the beginning is worse than pitiful? Actually non-existent if you're honest about your expenses.

16. Might you be better off staying with your regular job and writing for pleasure and more of a sideline, rather than boarding the runaway train of authoring, publishing, building your platform, mar-

keting, learning technologies, strategizing, accounting, and tackling the barrage of chores that ambush writer/publishers?

17. Finally, what about living arrangements? Do you have children who need an attentive parent? Do you have a significant other who deserves a memo about where you're headed? They all should prepare for the breadth of this before you sail off with bestsellers in your eyes. A best-case scenario is that your 'other' loves your writing, believes in you, and wants what you want for yourself. You could be lucky and have a real helper, someone even willing to assist with research, blog-reading, accounting, God knows what. Many lovers and spouses are dependable beta-readers (ones who test-read books before they're released), as well as proofreaders, even editors. Not to mention they serve you snacks, sit beside you at the keyboard, and massage your neck at 2 a.m. If you possess this human asset, you're blessed. Next best is a partner who maybe doesn't picture themself by your side accepting Pulitzer Prizes, but at least doesn't take offense at your new obsession.

Just know you ain't gonna be the binge-watching love panda you were. And a life partner should be clued in. So s/he can bail.

The more you delve into these questions and their answers, the clearer you'll be. But doing the heave-ho of an entire team will add all new dimension to the concept of overwhelm. However, with a mind-set that it will be novel, exciting, educational, rewarding, demanding, and even fun some of the time, you'll be at least mentally prepared.

Do I feel bad confiding all this? I do. That's why no one else tells the truth about it. But I've stayed with it, despite everything, and I'll share that, too. It's by no means misery. Making books cover-to-cover is richly creative, totally consuming, highly satisfying, and a lasting accomplishment.

✕✕

Okay, stage set. What next? We're moving forward, terrified, but stoked. We're clear on the sacrifices. We accept there isn't much middle ground in this gig—you either do one or two books and sell a few dozen or at most one or two hundred, or forget life as you've known it and commit to a rigorous, slow-to-materialize entrepreneurship as an author, publisher, PR person, accountant, and…lone wolf.

So, expand your desk, get some new file boxes and folders, a good lamp, give yourself elbow room, and make sure you're content in the space you'll be sitting in for the next few years. (Although, I will add here that, despite the scale of what you're em-barking on, another major perk is that your pub-lishing business will be surprisingly compact and portable.)

XOXOXOX

- 5 -

PRINT BOOKS VS. EBOOKS

Still reading?? Good. You're tough.

Okay, so if you're writing/publishing books for the money, I don't even know what to say to you. Was Leonardo da Vinci in it for the money? Rembrandt? Bob Dylan? The Beatles? Dear Ernie Hemingway?

Most of us associate art with the desire to make something out of nothing, to make something meaningful out of something difficult or complicated or vague. Recycling emotion. You've got your story and you need it to be a book…. Therefore, this conversation is primarily about print books. Of course, you'll have an ebook, too, but this book is geared toward paperback books to hold in the hands. As a veritable author, don't you want your book in print?

Personally, it never entered my mind to only have ebooks. When I'm writing books, I'm creating something to read in bed or get lost in on the plane. Or to read outside under the old oak tree. You pull it out, feel its cover, read the back cover, and there's

33

even a little dreaming and yearning as interest and excitement creep in. You can't wait to open and discover this book you now own. I had zero interest in writing a book that would never be in paperback.

But…let's suppose you really are a one-book wizard. Nearly everyone has a story to tell — a life story or some epic segment of a life. If this is you, I seriously don't recommend mastering publishing. Save up ten grand, get a night job for six months or a year, and commission it. Google some publishing companies, even small ones (there are scores), then either pass off your whole book to one of them, or do it a la carte, selecting your own editors, formatters, proofreaders, and cover designers. You can even go to Fiverr.com and piecemeal your project together on a slim budget. Let others construct your book while you focus on the story. Self-publishing, done properly, is too much exertion for just one book, plus the first book is by far the hardest.

Now, if you don't mind never having a paperback, an ebook is definitely easier and cheaper. And having just one book to publish is one example of when an ebook might be your best option.

Another example of when you might do just an ebook is THIS book. If your book isn't long, or if you don't expect it to be relevant ten years from now, you can still get your message out. But I'll still do a paperback version of this.

So there are legitimate reasons to do just an ebook. A good one is to save money. Another is it's simpler. One more might be to earn a little money due to having fewer expenses. Or maybe you want to test the waters with a book idea. Or you want to knock out something fast, to have it quickly for sale on line in time for some occasion. I'd say the main three reasons are: cheaper, faster, and much easier. But you'll never hold the real book in your hands.

For our purposes here, we're largely talking print books. By the same token, when publishing, you'll want the ebook edition, as well — it's nuts not to. Once you've done the heavy lifting, ebooks are gravy.

- 6 -

HOPE YOU LIKE PYRAMIDS

Let me address something you must grasp right from the start.

Even though all the blogs tell you how important the marketing part of publishing is, it's not until you set your book afloat in the vast ocean of commerce and competition that the 'self' part of publishing hits home. You've been wholly consumed with first writing your book, then mastering publishing. You've been somersaulting through website creation, bios, book descriptions, ISBN, meta data, Library of Congress, editing, formatting, cover design, choosing from the options for printing and distribution…. Now your book is out there, literally trying to swim to China.

Silly you, you thought finishing the book was the hard part. Like all authors, you believed the merit of the book — lively writing, unique information, and/or strong story — would be compelling enough that everyone who read it would naturally recommend it to their friends and/or associates. Then you'd have some book-signings to generate more interest and, next thing you knew, Terry Gross at NPR would be phoning for an interview.

Just a few pieces missing from these expectations. One is the misconception about compounded readership. Ten good friends reading your book, even loving it, don't mean each will get even one of their friends to buy and read it. If you're phenomenally lucky, one of your ten will possibly get their husband or child to read it. But they'll lend them their copy, meaning you won't even garner a new sale.

Consider multi-level marketing, the pyramid schemes we're all familiar with. Ever try to lasso in some pals or the gang at your hair salon so you can make money off the tier below you? If so, you know it's not only a hard sell, but painful. And even if you reel someone in, you then have to badger that poor soul incessantly so s/he gets recruits. It's funky, phony, and obnoxious. But the pyramid is not an a-similar model for the one-on-one promotion required to sell our books. The absolute first person I ever questioned about how self-publishing works told me bluntly, "You have to shamelessly promote yourself."

Doing anything shamelessly is counter-intuitive and awkward beyond measure. But, once you master the physical publishing, promoting is the next beast to confront.

So, do you even bother touting your work of art to your circle of close friends and relations? Certainly! They're your biggest fans. But realize they're not 'the market.' People who love you, regardless of your talent (or lack of), may readily purchase your book, and perchance even post an Amazon review, but that's all. They won't be talking it up around town, blogging about it, or buying ten copies for everyone at the office. Well, Mom might; from the rest, the very most you can hope for is an on-line review. And we'll get to those shortly.

So, what about freebies, giveaways, and gaining visibility? Tactics to draw in readers. (Again, I'm talking about paperbacks, though your book is probably also in ebook.) Well, I don't know about you, but I believe my books are worth reading. 'Worth' reading — not just the time it takes to read one, but the price one pays to do so. So I don't hand them out like flyers or business cards. I sell them.

XOXOXOX

– 7 –

GETTING PREPARED

Here are some preparatory factors to keep in mind:

1. EVER-CHANGING. The self-publishing industry is fluid. Stay abreast of news, opportunities, transitions, and trends. For example, this book is being published in April 2019, and was written and re-edited over the past couple of years, yet, as mentioned, things keep shifting. Some details I'm covering may have changed by the time you read this, and more will later on.

2. ENDLESS COMBINATIONS OF STRATEGIES. Although I have scoured and continue to track nearly all the self-publishing resources up, down, sideways, backwards, inside out, and in cir-

cles, that's not to say there aren't better or other ways to do this (or will be). There are myriad avenues and combinations of approaches that I, personally, didn't choose for my books. I can't encourage you enough to formulate an approach that suits YOU, that fulfills your ambitions, that you can afford, and that makes you feel satisfied. Because the frustration of self-publishing can be almost insurmountable at times. Look what happened to poor Ernest Hemingway. (There also may come a time to just break open that piggy bank and hire a first-responder.)

3. LEARN THE TECHNOLOGY. Don't be terrified of or resistant to technology. It may seem kind of like fixing your car—the idea of all that grease. Self-publishing isn't radically different from 'DIY Auto Mechanics for Those with No Clue.' The notion of all those inexplicable pieces attached to each other is beyond daunting. To decide you're just not going there is understandable. But then you either won't get your books published or you'll pay serious moola for someone else to do your mud wrestling. And it all comes back to you anyway—choosing who to hire; making decisions about editing, formatting, and cover; submitting your bio and blurbs; developing an email list; courting social media; studying marketing; notating your accounts; writing the next book(s); and all-around entrepreneurialism. Might as well just boot up your caffeine habit and jump in.

But it's technical, and you won't survive if you're squeamish about alien stuff like InDesign, website building, Adobe Illustrator, YouTube channels, social media, you name it. You don't have to do all of it, but you definitely have to do some of it.

4. COVER ALL YOUR BASES. To reiterate, there are essentially three main methods of self-publishing. A) Hire other people to do the serious publishing and the follow-through for you — recommended if you've got scratch. But paying back these costs from eventual earnings can mean years or forever before you turn a profit. B) Do all you can on your own, and commission out the elements that truly seem beyond your skill-set, time-frame, or willingness to learn. C) Bite the bullet and say, "Okay, maybe it's greasy, maybe it's foreign to me, maybe it's not my strong suit or my inclination, maybe I don't feel like it, but I **can** conceivably do this."

It's not actually that hard, just intimidating and relentless, but you **CAN** do it. The good news is that it isn't greasy, you'll arrive with clean fingernails. But any single aspect you skip over is like saying, "I'll learn this language, but not the verbs," or "I love this car, but I'm never changing the oil." Anything you neglect to look into will bite you in the butt — you'll make mistakes and miss ways to either produce a better book or make more money.

And if you stay in the game, you'll end up revisiting all of it with your next book(s) anyway. You'll be saying things like, "You know what, I didn't get the digital rights, I didn't get the global rights, I didn't own my ISBN number, I published too quickly, my book needed more edits. Or I quoted song lyrics without authority, I didn't include drawings that needed to be there, I had a half-baked cover, I used real people's names, I didn't have it proof-read, I didn't acknowledge people who helped me." And more. So cover the bases.

If you believe you've got a riveting book or several in you, research your options extensively before publishing.

5. SET UP A DISCIPLINED ROUTINE. In this occupation, you'll get carried away at times and be really glued to your computer. So, while taking on publishing, you must also create a decent physical regimen — exercise, enough sleep, nutritious food and drink. (I personally don't believe one can publish books without caffeine, but prove me wrong.) Just be forewarned that, if you're worn to a frazzle, your exasperation will be heightened. But if you're getting quality time elsewhere — walks or swims, frolicking with pets, laughing with friends, dating cute people, getting your zzz's, and Dancing With the Stars — then you won't be swallowed whole because you'll know how to step

away from the writing/publishing world. I can't emphasize this enough.

6. A LOT OF HYPE OUT THERE. I know I'm painting a grim picture, I just feel it has to be done. I can't tell you how tired I am of blog post headings like, "Have a NY Times Bestseller," "Find Your First 5,000 Readers," "14 EASY Marketing Tips," "Get Your Book in Costco and Walmart," and "Promote Your Book on 'Good Morning America'!" Sure, I've opened these emails, mainly because there can be invaluable educational tips baiting us in, but all the sender ultimately wants is for you to buy their book or their course.

Btw, *this* book is *not* an ad. Though you can buy my other books should you care to, I won't be pitching a webinar a few pages from here. And I'm not a writing coach. Nor am I writing 'Surviving Self-Publishing' for my ego or to make money. I'm writing it because I didn't find this vein of discourse anywhere when combing the net for how all this works (or doesn't). It took me a ludicrous amount of stumbling to find my way to published books.

I couldn't find anything not only because no one wants to be the party-pooper bursting every wanna-be's balloon, not only because no one wants to blow the lid off the myth that self-publishing is a walk in the dark—oops, I mean park, but because this industry can be misleading and play on people's dreams. Bloggers gloss over the struggle because their incomes derive from services and products new authors can and do purchase.

Who doesn't want to write a book and be an author? There's a veritable army to be lured down the lane of envisioning oneself a published author selling stacks of books. Bestsellers! Nearly everyone has given it a thought at some point. So self-publishing is made to seem exciting and profitable.

I mean, balloons are okay; and no one wants to be the one saying, "You ain't leaving the ground, kid." But someone needs to prepare you.

7. ADJUST YOUR TIME-FRAME AND IN-COME EXPECTATIONS. When I look back at my goals and projections from the first couple of self-publishing years, man was I off the mark. The time estimations for books sold, total earnings, and new books to be released were off by about a decade. Maybe two. I'm serious. You might compare it to marrying or having a child — the reality just isn't like you pictured. Where's the glamour? Where's the sense of arrival and victory? Where'd all this drudgery come from? Why am I so tired and frustrated?

I've found, through the years, that when we're deeply, energetically involved in making something happen, we're usually not even aware of our progress yet—we're so busy. Self-publishing's no different. You'll get somewhere in time, but you may hardly notice any milestones along the way because you're so hell-bent on grappling with the next challenge on your checklist.

As a rule of thumb, I'd add no less than two or three years to your expectations about how much you can get done as a publisher. This includes how long it takes to finish writing a book, how long to prepare a book for publishing, how long to launch a book, how long to market a book, and how long to see sales and income worth mentioning. This is a business of building. You're constructing products and a brand from the ground up, working your learning curve as a publisher/marketer, and attracting a reader base. Your identity is morphing as you try different approaches and master obtuse skills. Like any massive goal initially out of reach, it takes time to inch toward it. If your heart is in it, dig in for the long haul, re-adjusting your expectations and dreams. Then knuckle under.

※※※※※

- 8 -

GOING PUBLIC

For me, going public was so life-threatening I started off with a pen-name. Then again, I was writing memoir, maybe your genre's less personal....

People who write a lot are, by definition, somewhat private — privacy and quiet being requirements for collecting and recording one's thoughts. You depend on ample, unstructured time to transfer feelings, ideas, stories, and info onto the page, and sweet serendipity to validate or jump-start the process. You need your mornings, nights, or long afternoons, and you don't want to talk about it or explain how it comes together for you, it just does. You really don't have a lot of choice about all this.

But the publishing side is different. And this comes as a jolt to a cave-dweller. It's a nine-to-nine job — takes heaps of tangible labor that's got to get done. And you're disturbingly aware that the longer it takes, the more years will be added to the dawning of your success.

So you take it on. At least you're slaving over your own material and you're at home, in the security of your lair. Even though you're fatter now from sitting at your desk 24/7.

But then...just when you have absolutely *no time* for anything else, because you're so snowed under by all there is to do as a writer/publisher/marketer, now you have to go out and...get a life?

"What?! Why? I have a (cerebral) life, I'm a writer."

No, you have to step out. You HAVE to. Not just to shamelessly promote your books, but because you can't succeed in-hiding. You've got to interact with the world, for your mental health if nothing else. And you've got to maybe buy a selfie-stick and do some videos, get some decent photos of yourself. You've also got to appear happy one way or another because there's nothing interesting about a slug in a bathrobe.

You have to. You need some light in those eyes, oxygen in those veins. You need input from the outside world to counter-balance all that's pouring out of you every day. Coffee and muffins will not help you here. You've got to create balance so you can go the distance. You've got to up the heart-rate, take breaks from the grind. Otherwise, going public is too freaky — not because you don't look good, but because you don't feel good *and* you don't look good.

There's also the issue of whether you WANT the big bad world inside your personal domain. In the old days, being a writer was an invisible walk of life—no one knew where you lived, what you looked like, how old you were, or whether you wore moose slippers. Writers were nebulous creatures behind the scenes, kind of like puppeteers. And the mystique was respected. People simply read your books and looked forward to the next one.

Today an author is a brand. If you have more than one book, you yourself are part of the package. Thanks to the good ol' Internet, you're expected to provide illustrative, tasty morsels as to who you are and what you're up to—the more intriguing, accessible, humorous, colorful, or down-home, the better. And, ironically, the more of your books people read, the less they want to envision you stuck in a chair somewhere. So, it's worth taking up spelunking to fluff up your bio. Or go to far-off lands for far-fetched reasons— they love that. As a marketeer now, don't withhold anything that might increase revenue. But, okay, if 'fat and ugly' is your default persona and you live in a flannel onesy, then show us pictures and let us laugh at you.

You can't be fake either. (Well, you can, and everyone is to an extent, but yuck.) No, you've got to be authentic, and that feels dicey, because we, ourselves, are usually the ones with the least inkling who we truly are and how to present our je ne sais quoi.

So you have to fumble your way into that. You have to learn to describe yourself and act like you're completely comfortable just being wonderful you.

Definitely meditate on this. There's no getting around it.

XOX

Now, if anyone's still reading after those last two points, I think the next preparation piece is three-pronged: 1) being yourself, 2) having fun, 3) marketing.

We'll be talking about points 1 and 2 a bit later, because they might be the truest keys to 'success' (hate to even use that sketchy word), but let's address number 3.

Marketing is complex. Thankfully, countless blog-posts cover every angle of it. After comprehensive research, you carve your own path through the jungle. However, savvy selfers all concur that developing an email list is paramount. Again, there's plenty out there on this topic. But I, too, suggest you immediately begin collecting email addresses from anyone who may be a reader of your book(s). Be realistic, of course, about who will resonate with your material. You don't want a 500-person email list of fourth-graders from the school where you teach and cab-drivers from your trip to Egypt. Think genre reader, avid reader, niche reader, or curious reader.

Don't worry about the size of your list, it will grow as your author existence does. But start using your list right away — regardless of how few names are on it. Let them know when books come out, where to buy them, and other pertinent, enthralling data. You want them to purchase your books, enjoy them, and review them. But this takes muscle. Shameless muscle. Because no one parts easily with their time and money. Also, even though your list is a marketing device, you can't bombard your tribe with pleas to buy books. You have to apply some charm by spiking interest, humoring them, or bribing them.

It's wide open what you can do. But your list will be your principle tool for attracting both buyers and reviewers. It's the one thing you can depend on and use on your own terms and your own schedule. And it's personal. These contacts are in many ways your friends, because they've shown interest in what you're doing and have *given* you their data.

XOXOXOX

- 9 -

REVIEWS

Now is an opportune moment to discuss reviews. The most basic ways to secure on-line reviews are as follows:

1. Prime acquaintances before they buy your book, "If you like it, please write a review on Amazon."

2. Make sure you have their email address so you can follow up.

3. If you're selling someone a book face to face, offer them a discount should they agree (that is, they swear to God on a stack of bibles) to write a review. Avid readers will snatch up the deal—

they're addicts—often extrapolating on how profi-
cient they are at review writing. But unless you dog
them diligently, you'll never see that review. "Why?
Did they hate the book?" Probably not. (You made
sure it was stupendous before you published it,
right?) Naa, they've just moved on to the next book
they impulsively bought. "Well, how do I know
they even read my book?" You don't. It could still
be sitting on the bottom of their night-table stack.
"But what if they hated it and that's why they didn't
write a review?" Doubtful that's the reason; it just
wasn't on their to-do list, and they forgot about it.
You didn't badger them enough. "I think they hate
me." No, they liked meeting you, but that was weeks
ago in a leisurely moment—now they're back to the
grind.

Welcome to author life, you'll get used to it.

4. If you know a certain individual bought
your book or even was given it by someone, email
them a 'thank you in advance for reading it,' and
mention how you cherish reviews. Then allow them
time to read the book (weeks, sometimes months,
sometimes never).

5. Follow up, asking if they enjoyed the book
and, if so, requesting the review. If they need a boost,
offer to assist with their review or even help them
craft it over the phone. I know it sounds pathetic, but

readers aren't necessarily writers—what's simple for us can be a tall order for someone else.

6. Offer to aid the technically-impaired with the posting of their reviews. Amazon doesn't make the process 'for dummies.' At the time of this writing, Amazon requires any reviewer to have made a purchase of at least $50 within the past year through that same Amazon.com account.Your book needn't have been part of it or even purchased through Amazon. They just insist reviewers be actual Amazon customers in some capacity.

7. Thank reviewers profusely if they actually comply. Most will not. Don't take it personally.

8. Hear what they are saying. Maybe they didn't like the book and don't want to lie or hurt your feelings. Go after the ones who loved it or who love you, and who don't have review-itis. Remind them that their review doesn't have to be elaborate or long, doesn't have to be five stars, and they can even use an alias. All your readers will smile, nod, and assure you they'll submit the review, but they will not. That's why there are all sorts of scams, payment methods, and harsher new Amazon regulations. Reviews are a big issue for the Zon, a big issue for authors, and a big issue for readers—everyone is emotionally and financially affected by them.

So what do you do?

Beg.

In the politest possible way, shamelessly persist.

You won't regret it, because the wonderful news is, in the exceptional instance you actually score a review, it stays with your book indefinitely. A good review is 'the gift that keeps on giving.' Especially if you plan to publish more than one book, the absolute best thing you can do, aside from writing great stuff, is to train some of your readers to automatically post reviews whenever they finish one of your books. I have about two people trained now.

Another indirect way to play up the importance of reviews is to effusively thank "all who've written reviews" in an email to your whole list—hoping the others might catch review fever. But they never do.

XOXOXOX

- 10 -

EXPOSURE, GIFTING, AND PRICING

What follows was not suggested to me by anyone else nor condoned anywhere. But…I, generally, do not gift my books.

"What?! Why not?"

Three reasons:

1. I'm in business. Profits are already so ridiculous that if I'm passing out books willy-nilly, I might as well forget about income altogether. For many authors, this paltry difference in chump change may not be a factor, but from the start and to this moment, in April 2019, my goal has been to put out numerous books and generate higher income each year. I'm in this for years to come.

Ava Greene

I know there's a lot of noise about 'exposure' and how having your books scattered around offers visibility you'd not otherwise have. Libraries are the perfect example. Any library anywhere will take a free copy of your book. Sure, why not? But any residual benefit or 'exposure' really can't be effectually measured. What's tangible is that you just bought that book from your printer for probably $3 to $7, had it shipped for maybe $.40 per copy, and you drove to that library at least once, probably two or three times, in order to schmooze with the appropriate librarian to set up this fabulous arrangement. If you make glad-handing a habit, you'll soon run out of not just books but belief in your author identity.

To the contrary, if one out of five libraries actually BUYS your book, you tally up that sale in your ledger, add it to this month's earnings, and see how it compares to this time last year. Libraries, btw, have hearty acquisition budgets and can afford to buy the books. Why not wow them into a sale? And their lending system for ebooks remunerates authors surprisingly well, so why forego that opportunity? Wow them.

Judge 'gifting' and 'exposure' for yourself. For me, though, the bottom line is the bottom line. I can rationalize, dream, pretend, and spend money all year long in the name of visibility or exposure, but monetary success is tallied by how many books

I SELL and at what price. Sales are what will keep me publishing and marketing, not knowing my donations have been quietly moved to forgotten back shelves of suburban libraries around my county or my country (after I shipped them in). I record my expenses religiously, including shipping and taxes and giveaways, and one way to get a leg up is to lower such costs. In business, income is what matters—ask any Shark.

Ditto for consignment—unless it's a high-profile, easily accessible book store or gift shop where it's practically assured you'll sell books. In that case, it might conceivably be worth the hassle and possible fee they often charge to have your books displayed in their 'Local Authors' or 'Self-Published' section. But it will still be your responsibility to make sure enough of your books are there; to track how many they've sold; to collect your pay; to check that your books are properly displayed; to remove any getting dusty, faded, or shabby from handling; and to cozy up to the store's workers in hopes they'll recommend your titles.

Another factor is, once you start giving books away, where do you draw the line? So, as a general rule (with exceptions), I don't donate and don't do consignment. I do, however, readily knock off a couple of bucks for friends, clients, and nearly all in-person sales. "Get a signed copy from me right now and I'll give you two dollars off." And to coax readers further, into maybe buying one or two more of my titles right now, I might lower the prices even more. "Buy more than one book, and we'll make it three dollars off per book."

Some writers will trade other authors for their books, agreeing to write mutual reviews. This is your call. I've tried it a few times. Do you really want to read and review some random book you've just exchanged for yours? I don't, it's drudgery—most self-published books don't fully deliver, I'm sorry to say. Then I'm stuck having to write a false good review. But that's just me; call me a snob; I like an inspiring or fun read. And, again, since you've paid for this book you're handing off, you've had it shipped, and you've stored it in a box in your closet or garage, wouldn't you rather sell it?

On the other hand, trading books for auto repair or handyman services can be a happy win-win. And this is someone you know (and you're THEIR customer), so you might just get that coveted review.

2. My no-freebie policy was actually underscored when I first started publishing. I'd occasionally gift books as a thank you when I'd been a house-guest, or as a sign of appreciation to someone. Guess what? Receivers of gift books didn't read them! Sometimes they even managed to lose them. Yet those who paid ALWAYS read them.

So I'll offer my discounts to my buyers. Absolutely — I adore these people. And everyone loves a deal. But I'm not trying to lure in bottom-feeders or draw in readers who are searching for the cheapest reading material this side of the Continental Divide. I'm a hardworking author selling fine stories at a fair price. Plenty of readers still get excited about authors and fresh new books. There's actually magic in it, because everyone has a story but few write it, fewer write it well, and fewer still offer numerous good books.

3. Third, by gifting books, you may undermine yourself. It's weird psychology, but in business you have to draw boundaries. Even just for your own record-keeping or ease of operation, you have to decide what you're worth, when you'll discount, when you won't, and exactly what your prices are. Things can get fuzzy if you don't have a constitutional framework. Granted, you may lower your prices as you write more books, as your sales grow higher across the boards and maybe costs are lessened, too. And, no doubt, you'll run ads and special offers. But your overall process, year after year, will be easier when you've defined, to yourself and others, what's expected. Quality, consistency, and confidence are what make a notable brand. My darling grandmother, a peerless dressmaker in New York City, who grew an impressive clientele out of nothing and stayed in that métier right up to her death at 86, used to say, "Put

a price tag on yourself and never go down for a bargain." As a teenager, I shrugged off that advice (probably because I wasn't selling anything so it seemed a bit vague), but I now understand she excelled in her field by attaching top value to her craftsmanship, her originality, her expertise, and her time. She knew where her prices had to be to remain motivated to labor as hard as she did. As an author, you're not going to get enough money anyway, no matter what you do, but you can know your authordom has backbone. (Funny, isn't it, how the advice of long-deceased relatives echoes throughout our days?)

So, what price do you charge for your book?

Pricing something always involves algorithms, and the determinants for mine have been threefold:

1. What is the realistic price-range for a book of this length and genre?

2. How much do I need to make per book—not even deducting all my overall publishing costs, but deducting the printing cost of each book—that will allow me to be honest with myself about how much or how little I'm earning? It's too tragic to admit to ourselves, let alone anyone else, if we're making zilch per book or, worse, if each sale is actually a *cost*.

3. After doing my research, have I lowered my costs per book as much as humanly possible to create

improved monetary margins? For example, in my first book, I didn't realize that the publisher (me) pays a few pennies for each blank page in a book. When selling hundreds or thousands of copies, it's worth tightening up your formatting. Like, in a 'perfect' book, each chapter would begin on a right-hand (recto) page, but understanding book space as real estate, in my second book I let my chapters begin on whichever side they naturally spilled out, saving me about twenty-six blank pages. Those twenty-six blank pages would've cost me around $.50 per book, also increasing each book's shipping weight. Over months and years, that's extra cost you don't want, because it means you'll either make less profit for each sale, have to charge more for that title, or just eat it and end up with not a business but an interesting-but-disappointing author experience.

Just my opinions, at this stage of my own trek. And, like I said, this doesn't apply to advertising deals, something that probably will become part of your repertoire when you have a few books and some positive reviews kickin' around. But I can't reiterate enough how every author is different, so do what you feel! And, hey, by all means, if money's no object, you're on a different roller coaster altogether. Or maybe you're 93 years old…. Play it your way!

XOXOXOX

- 11 -

GET DEPRESSED AND THEN GET OVER IT

It wouldn't be fair to ignore something that can pop up any time and will more than once. I'm including this because it's inevitable. However, it's possible you haven't hit the wall yet. Sorry, you will. I'm pretty sure all authors do, including traditionally-published ones. But let's stay with the indie scenario.

We start out full of questions. We do a bunch of research. Ultimately, we decide to go for it and publish a book—with the clear understanding there's no clear understanding as to what we're getting into. We've decided it's doable and we're up for the challenge. We've concluded that we can afford whatever level of professional help we *can* fiscally afford. Hopes and dreams, btw, are probably the best fuel in the world — they can last half a lifetime, against all odds, even against all common sense.

But, at some point, the honeymoon with becoming an author will wind down. The undertaking has been more convoluted, complicated, technically exhausting, financially laughable, crazy demanding, and short on accolades than you ever anticipated. And so s-l-o-w you've shredded this year's goals. Plus there's no end in sight — you're now either in for the marathon, ready to jump ship, or so blitzed on pharmaceuticals and sad about the divorce that nothing matters anymore.

These segues from dream to plan to cataclysmic workload to grueling perseverance take some time. But, tactically, our hopes and dreams just have to be re-vamped into something less grandiose, less frilly, less lucrative.

Okay, fine.

But about that same time, we're also accumulating months and years of hands-on experience, and there's no substitute for that. We're not exactly rich and famous, and we're discerning that 'being a writer' isn't what people think. However…we have a published book, we're authors, we've done it, we've gotten some reviews, and this stuff feels pretty righteous.

I actually think some reflective time is essential. We get real with ourselves and ask hard questions: "Is this worth all the work?" "Seriously, is it?" "How strong am I?" More importantly, we re-evaluate our relationship to our writing, our books, our careers, our families, our health, and our mental stability. We renew our vows with our cats.

One thing I remain uncomfortable with is that most of the bloggers who cover self-publishing seem to be under oath or something to not address the negatives. Or maybe as American 'rugged individualists,' we're all groomed to never give up, never back down, don't stop believin'. True, in this country there's always a fresh entrepreneurial quest waiting to replace any that dissolve into grated Parmesan. But I'm six and a half years into this and little of my expedition has been what I thought, wanted, envisioned, expected, was told, or deemed myself capable of. I'd even like to slap an inspirational sentence onto the end of this paragraph, but I'm not under oath and I'm not going to.

I'll just say I am tougher now, I'm more tech-savvy than probably anyone in my demographic, I'm getting the hang of this, I'm used to having no life, and I look forward to the day when I've totally tamed the dragon. (Getting close!) Plus, I have four published paperbacks and ebooks (and this one) under my name and pen-name; and my poetry collection, my 'Nicaragua Story,' and my first audio books are on the way. But are waves of applause rolling in? Has NPR phoned? Are fans clambering for my next book?

Ava Greene

I think you really have to supply those pats on the back yourself, isn't that weird? But isn't all of life a little weird? Don't glory and praise and the rush of achievement spring up where and when you least expect them?

One soothing little ritual I picked up from Jeff Walker, a product-launch marketer with a friendly philosophy, is to acknowledge my wins each day before I drift off to sleep. It helps to recognize that neat and fruitful things do happen every single day.

But am I excited about the bookkeeping that continually adding more paperbacks, ebooks, and audio books to my line-up will entail? Am I thrilled that having translations in foreign countries will further complicate my accounting? Is there enough time in life to produce all the books I could conceivably offer? Enough time to review all my back pages and compile everything into viable manuscripts? Can I continue to brazenly promote myself to my email list? Am I comfortable spending money on advertising? (Getting there....) Will ads pay off?

Who knows? But I'm staying the course. Gutsiness has always served me in the long run. Though I usually travel by tightrope getting there.

All those questions are *depressing*. But, periodically, I do entertain them. Can't imagine any author who doesn't. But then…I re-group. I commend myself for my efforts and accomplishments. I supply my own cheering section. I look at my goals and journal entries from the year(s) before and acknowledge how far I've come. I realize I have author appearances scheduled on my calendar now when I didn't before. I fondly thumb through my published books. I write in my journal. I edit a current manuscript. I ameliorate the cover design for my next book. I re-read my stellar Amazon reviews. I talk through my issues on my phone recorder and listen back weeks later. I build my audio recording space. I vent to someone. I go to the beach. I eat better food. I do my yoga. I take a trip. I write. I go spelunking. I search for Big Foot.

And I continue on my path. It's the one I've chosen, and there's tons more work to do.

And every year I seem to reach new volumes in sales, I attain new levels by following the steps and advise in blogs, my author stature increases with more books written and more notches in my publishing belt. And I pinch myself and look skyward as it settles in that my books are good books, and I'm doing and being what I wanted and needed to do and be.

Ava Greene

P.S. Then you get a three-sentence email like this one I opened at 5 am this morning:

"I wanted you to know I LOVVVVVVVED your most recent creation!!!! 'Expedition Costa Rica' was a through and through treasure to read, beautiful in every way and a tremendous journey of incredulous amazement. I will write something on Amazon this weekend."

And, by gum,, she did.

XOXOXOX

- 12 -

BRIEF NOTE ABOUT
MARKETING

Question: How long do you have to market your books?

Answer: As long as you want people to buy them.

More hard truth. But please take it seriously. If you can't or don't wish to generate excitement about your book, you'll likely have to be content with severely limited sales. But you'll still, at least, have a published book to your name!

So, even though I've learned a bit about marketing books, and have pursued numerous avenues—including 1) the Internet, book stores, libraries, book-signings, author talks, personal sales, and romancing my email list, 2) 'going wide' and making my books available on line in paperback and ebook all over the globe, including translations and audio (in the works), and 3) book tours, discounts, advertising, and events—I still don't consider myself a marketeer.

Marketing, I think, is really phase three, with writing as phase one, and publishing as phase two. Marketing's one more behemoth to wrangle. But this only becomes obvious as we add more products/books to the marketplace. Even with only a few books out, I've already seen how adding a new one enhances the others, and how they work as a group. But there are methods for leveraging products, as well as advertising psychology, timing of discounts and deals, and the testing of strategies. Phase three is an advanced and necessary approach to selling, mainly for determined authors with at least two titles and possibly more in the pipeline.

XOXOXOX

- 13 -

BE YOURSELF
AND HAVE FUN

A couple of years back, in readying my second book for release ('I Did Inhale — Memoir of a Hippie Chick'), I got bushwhacked by a combination of fear about the personal nature of the book, overwhelm re: all the marketing schemes that bloggers were touting, and boggled by the intricacies of InDesign (that I taught myself), Adobe Photoshop (that I taught myself), Adobe Illustrator (that I taught myself), cover template guidelines, and website updating. Simultaneously, I was grappling with customer service at Ingram Spark in Tennessee (they've now increased their hours and locations), BookBaby in New Jersey (they've now increased their hours and locations, but I'm no longer with them), HostBaby (for websites, in California), and Amazon's Author Central (in Costa Rica and India), all the way from Kaua'i where I reside, with its 3-6 hour time differential. Here I was, publishing my flagship book that I'd worked on a mere 38 years — it was like going down the aisle or having a first child — and I was a blurry, caffeinated mess getting downright angry at the whole self-publishing community for intimating I could do all this by myself!

Underneath it all, I believed in my book and needed to release it.

That's when I admitted I wasn't having fun. And that my principle had always been to enjoy life. And that it didn't make sense to slave this hard at anything that brought only anxiety, diminishing health, isolation, and frustration. Finding Big Foot would be kids' stuff compared to this.

I took a step back. I was reading this or that blog, listening to this or that webinar about all the ways to promote and sell books, and it became suddenly clear that one single individual couldn't possibly do even half of it! So I took off the rosy glasses, looked at these bloggers and webinar hosts more critically, and came clean that I'm not *them*. My books aren't like theirs, my goals aren't like theirs, my reality isn't like theirs. Plus I'm out in the middle of the Pacific Ocean, for cripes' sake. I can't do things the way they would, so I'm not going to.

That was a breath of fresh air. I stopped pumping so hard. I had more taped conversations with myself about how to make the process more pleasant and how to customize book-selling within a lifestyle I might resonate with. By then I'd swum through oceans of info and advice from those gone before me, and I'd published two books. But I wasn't out to make millions, I didn't yearn for a mansion and a Maserati, and I wasn't a 35-year-old male go-getter trying to attract a sexy woman to mother my children. Also, I wasn't striving for the financial freedom to one day escape to a tropical island out in the blue beyond, because I already did that.

I was decades into my life, had other gainful pursuits (that I cherished as a balance to the desk work, plus my clients buy my books); I already had about ten books all or partly written lined up for future publishing; Paradise was already right outside my door; I was comfy with my first-generation Prius; and I was happily married to my cat. I realized I had little in common with these self-pub mentors, whose accomplishments were far more about marketing and material acquisition than literary achievement. Some might be true writers at heart, but a bunch were really ad men and women, plain and simple.

So I broke from the ranks. It had to be more fun. I'd be creative, a little off-beat perhaps, and find my own ways of selling.

For me, this would probably mean traveling. I'd go to cities and states I was curious about, places I hadn't been yet, and where my flock might be hanging out. (I didn't advance that agenda right away because my travel at that time was always to visit my beloved, bedridden, 95-year-old dad 5600 miles away, but it was in the hopper.)

Along with tweaking my methods, I could also benefit from being a little older — I wasn't broke and my food-and-gas budget didn't hinge on book income. I had my other freelance occupation as well as a rental property, so even my long-term plan wasn't publish-dependent.

It was freeing to acknowledge I wasn't in the same league as these young broncos driven by financial success. All they blogged about was their empire-building and seven-figure winnings derived from email marketing, teaching courses to authors and other entrepreneurs, and the advantages of working with affiliates. Though they were clearly hard-working, and understood the writer quandaries, they had no interest in being authors. They were all about 'lifestyle' (previously known as 'wealth,' and before that as 'being filthy rich'). They constantly shook their fingers at marketing that was "sleazy," "cheesy," or "sales-y," yet theirs was worse. Many had no qualms emailing their list up to seven times in one day!! In their galaxy, this is acceptable marketing procedure.

Surviving Self-Publishing

I don't thumb my nose at them, per se, but I had to bring things down to earth for myself. My needs and desires are tied to writing and publishing books that entertain and inspire. I'd like my sales to grow as my new books are released. I don't need to get rich, I don't need bestsellers. What I do want are continuing good reviews.

You, too, must define your trajectory. Try to sense when and if it's time to re-configure your aims and goals, rethink your motivation, maybe take a breather and re-evaluate your deepest yearnings. As I said chapters back, no two authors will have the same game plan.

I sincerely recommend having sources of income other than book sales. The less pressure to make money at writing/publishing straight out of the gate, the better. Not feeling rushed lets you focus on value. And having outside income helps offset publishing costs. It also sponsors the hiring of help, advertising, or cash outlays for research and development of a book idea. Too, in having a day job, side hustle, or other ventures, you stay connected to the real world, the place where we stumble upon awesome material. Full-time writers can live in a box that isn't too picturesque and gives them bupkis to write about.

When book income's not the driving force, you're granted time — not just for re-writes, but to grow and explore as a writer and publisher. And the only way you can later 'murder your darlings' is to have darlings to murder. Where do you get them? They're birthed in the earlier years of honing the craft. (And if you've never heard that expression, another reason to hit the trenches a while and stream out your consciousness on the keyboard.)

For me, not being handcuffed to my computer is key to loving the pastime. The point isn't to 'be a writer,' but to write what I want and write well. Though I've been at it forever and now have published books, I've never seen the glory in 'being a writer' — something actually more like an addiction. I remember once a famous and glamorous man offered me a wing of his estate if I cared to move in, and my apologetic refusal was, "Y'know, I type a lot...." I was concerned about the noise, plus I didn't think he'd like being barred from that wing.

Now, at least I call it 'writing' rather than 'typing,' and at least it's quiet! But I never flaunt it. Unless there's a book sale in the offing. Writing is about the work, it's about the stories or the books, that's all. And it's about enjoying myself in the late hours of evening or early hours of morn, tapping away like some composer on a piano. It's never been about 'being a writer.'

So, claim a writer lifestyle that appeals to you. Don't get caught up in 'writer' clichés. And don't be in a rush. Just be yourself. Find original and light-hearted ways to promote your material. You'll be happier and so will your books.

As a writer, you can write whatever you wish, but as an author, your job is producing value for others—you've gone public. So don't do it for your ego, but as your contribution. Don't measure success solely by numbers of books sold—you'll need darned high digits to make a living at this, and outstanding luck in sustaining them. Judge your success by what your readers have to say.

- 14 -

BREAK YOUR ADDICTION TO HOW-TO MATERIAL

When commencing self-publishing, we're one hundred percent reliant on the Internet community for guidance, from the sequence of steps in the process, to where to find help, to mistakes to avoid, to where to flog our wares. The more we review what's available at what cost, the deeper we must dig to assure we haven't missed other options.

So you follow the blogs and soon your inbox is crawling with leads, offers, and free info, most of it fairly compelling. A hugely popular approach our gurus have is a free offer of real merit to entice us to a paid course or product they're promoting. Some of these coaches (who may later become a bit annoying) at first can be terrifically generous in what they share. So much so, that I've gathered planeloads of tips and instruction—everything from global marketing to landing pages to goal-setting to Amazon advertising to font choices to what goes into a media kit to how to sell to libraries to good websites to oh-you-name-it. Every single publishing decision was arrived at after endless Internet probes into fact-filled articles by experienced authors. In fact, the very purpose of this book is to supply one particular piece I didn't find on the information highway.

A well-spring of knowledge overflows from blogs and on-line commentary. These writers may be selling, but they treat other writers with respect because you're potentially their next client.

I've purchased some products over the years but, as useful as they seem, I don't always end up using them. I've also purchased two on-line courses from other mentors, at hundreds of dollars each, and have hardly used that material either, certainly not to the extent I intended to. So I'm more restrained now about paid guidance. But there's always tons to learn, and the leaders of the self-publishing field are crucial to the industry. They provide comfort, too, when you know not what comes next or there are dizzying choices.

Again, the writers' world is an articulate, thoughtful, succinct domain. Those who write about writing are obliged to do it well! It's even a cozy retreat sometimes to just surf the waters and see what peers are up to. (And sometimes these seasoned selfers can actually talk you down from the ledge.)

But watching webinars and perusing websites for infinite input can gobble up hours of your day. And eventually there comes a point when you have to be careful. Sure, most of it's relevant but, ultimately, you must pull back from these forums and get on with your mission. When you find yourself paying more attention to the Internet than your next book, surf back to shore. If not, all the on-line advice becomes distracting and your focus on it actually procrastination. You think you're researching when really you're recoiling from the next daunting task your work-in-progress is screaming for.

It's advantageous to keep up with industry changes, but at some point we plateau. Then, like a bird leaving the nest, we discover, perhaps with some nostalgia or hesitation, that we can fly on our own. The 'community' is no longer the go-to Oz it was, and we're more selective now in our on-line readings. Maybe that's when a true author identity starts to take shape…. You realize you're on your way, you've carved your own path through the factoid forest. You have a little history as a writer/publisher/marketer now, and some technical prowess. You've only gained 8.6 more pounds, and you even chime in occasionally in the comment sections. Best of all, you're still in the game!

XOXOXOX

- 15 -

FORGET ABOUT YOUR TIME-TABLE

About now, you can't help but notice that the time frames you'd slated for getting your books launched have been utterly and completely torched. I thought I'd have ten books out within the first three years; it's been over six now and my fifth and sixth books are w-a-y behind schedule.

But that launch calendar was incinerated long ago. Subsequent ones, too. In fact, each December or January, I re-write my book plans, and am re-stunned each year at how unrealistic my goals were. Every book has taken a good two years longer to launch than I expected. I can't even explain why. Could it be that other sectors of life take some of my time? All I know is that when

I look back at earlier iterations for cover concepts of a book, earlier drafts of texts, or earlier formatting choices, it's clear the books grew markedly better by taking the time to fine-tune things. Had I belabored over them even longer, who knows, my books probably would've continued to improve…. Books rarely get worse with another edit!

So, let go of release-dates scheduled back when. Books seem to be born and then become toddlers in your house as you're getting them ready to go to school. We're inclined to rush the process, but there's always more to do. Sometimes, even the last minute, we'll suddenly get a brilliant idea about how the book could be SO COOL. Now why would you cheat yourselves of making a book better? You can't! Even though the effort might push your launch back six months or even a year.

Months and years can feel like days and weeks in this pursuit. For example, with 'I Did Inhale — Memoir of a Hippie Chick,' the 335-page ditty I worked on three and a half decades…it was just about ready, cover all set, business cards made, website highlighting the new book, when I got the idea of interviewing the characters in the book as an epilogue. Since it was a true story, I thought it would be neat to read what some of my 'characters' had to say many years later about the wild times back then. I'd never seen that done in a book — making the concept all the more attractive. But of course it would take months to track down the real people from the book and either meet with them in person or have them send me something, and then compile it all.

I ended up with seven or eight contributors, and it did become my epilogue. It tied the book together well, even offering unexpected personal closure — but it took time…and you can't fight that.

Brake for the creative process.

But…as important as it is to wait till things are truly ready, it's equally timely to know when to let a book go, to let the baby birdie fly. This is an awkward and unfamiliar feeling, like a dad giving away the bride. "This feels too precarious…." But the time has come, and the precariousness adds to the power of the moment.

I may even have something of a blind spot regarding my final covers and final formatting choices, because once I get the real warm and fuzzies about how everything looks, I reach a point where I no longer want outside feedback. "Does this mean it's DONE?" I ask myself incredulously. It seems I could improve both interior and exterior forever, so it's counter-intuitive to quit seeking input. Yet I reach a sort of yield sign, a stopping place, where re-doing a cover or endlessly refining every possible element now seem like I'm just fussing, out of fear of letting the book go.

It's weird, because we're accustomed to *working* on a book, not to patting it on the head, wishing it the best of luck, and sending it out into the big, giant world all alone.

But the finish line's in sight. And that oddness is my green light to submit the files to the printer/distributor. Even though I know it will never be perfect. Now the focus will be on catching last-second, sneaky, little typos or flat-out errors that have somehow been overlooked. Believe me, they're there! (Mistakes and oversights eternally slip through, even in the slickest of traditionally-published books. Even in this book.)

So, set your goals—because goals are exciting and they give definition to career paths—but don't fret over them. And don't let them rule. The majority of self-published authors release books that aren't good enough, either because they didn't seek enough outside editing and feedback to fully craft the material, they believe books make money and they want some, they're so bent on 'being an author' that they'll sacrifice art in order to bang out product, or they're writing in hokey genres where quality's no concern. But don't ever believe quantity trumps quality. Never has, never will.

I mean, obviously, you're going to do what you want to do. But here's my take on it: if I'm going to bare my soul to the extent that I've got my name on hundreds of pages of personal content I'm sharing with the planet, it better be meritorious, well written, engage my readers from beginning to end, be worth their hard-earned money, and they better keep it on their bookshelf forever and blow kisses to it every time they saunter past.

Just keep putting one foot in front of the other. Don't beat yourself up over months dragging by. If you're making progress, you're making progress. It takes time to do this right. And I'm not even addressing the writing of these monsters — that's another conversation for another day. Just know from the start that publishing books correctly, books you'll be proud of now and later, takes way more time than you think. And 'perfection' isn't even in the equation.

XOXOXOXOX

- 16 -

GET DEPRESSED AND THEN GET OVER IT

Oh, I already said that.

"You mean get depressed *again* and then get over it *again*?"

Yup. Bound to happen.

My second bummer phase I think set in when it dawned on me how little money there is to be made at this. And how no one really told me that.

All those webinar-meisters, selling you the dream and rounding you up for their email lists, will *never* let on what a realistic expectation might be for a regular old author with a regular old book. Not to say your book isn't the next big thing, just that it's one of bazillions on the Amazon roster, and how does Joe-reader know how good it might be should s/he ever somehow stumble across it?

This next reality check banged me over the head when I went to Colorado because I got the bright idea that 'I Did Inhale' was highly thematic in a state that just legalized pot, and I could probably off-load dozens of books to stores there, maybe even to marijuana dispensaries. (Brilliant, no?) I reckoned even my other published book (I only had two titles then), 'Some Swamis are Fat,' might also sell in those 'high' altitudes. Plus my soon-to-be-released 'Expedition Costa Rica,' a macho adventure story, was also right up the hiking trail of that outdoorsy crowd.

So off I flew, as part of my have-fun-while-selling campaign. I like Colorado, had never been to Boulder, and would be flying right over on my way back from visiting Dad. It was my first selling mission outside my usual stops (Hawai'i, my Long Island hometown, and Venice, California — my former residence), so I had stars in my eyes and books in the trunk of my rental car.

But what I found out isn't going to make you very happy. I'd rather not even burst your indie bubble, though perhaps you've already been de-flowered by this prickly truth. I had dealt with it years earlier, but somehow spaced the datum until it road-blocked me in face-to-face meetings with buyers in notable Colorado book stores.

First I'll share what any pothead could've told me — people don't go to marijuana dispensaries for books. Catching sight of the prison-like entry doors and gender-certain 6′ 8″ security guards, I still remained buoyantly hopeful. Maybe inside everyone was kickin' back in overstuffed armchairs listening to Bob Marley and passing doobies around. "Hey, anyone in here wanna read my book?"

But the inside of these joints is anything but laid back. Picture a DMV for ex-cons—heavy regulation of the previously unregulated. Checking out three of those stores was sufficient reconnaissance to determine that my readers are not browsing in there.

As for book stores, I thought they'd be elated, or at least willing, to buy books directly from me. That way, they could save on shipping and have the books right away. But that's not how they do things….

Why not?

They can't. As in every industry, book stores doing brisk business use efficient systems for purchasing merchandise (to purch merch). Take Costco, just as an example of streamlined buying and selling. Imagine Costco buying five or ten books from little you. Not gonna happen. Why? You're not in their eco-sphere or in their computer, and their measly check to you wouldn't be recorded where their purchases need to be entered. But let's just say they do buy from you, and your critically-acclaimed 'How to Crochet Moose Slippers' sells out and they want to order more. Are they going to leave a message on your cell phone? "Hey, it's Jaymee at Costco. Can you drop off twelve more books on your next hummus run?" Think corporate, think colossal warehouse, reams of invoices, glazed office workers stoned on bargain cashews, freight containers full of frozen lasagna rumbling in on sixteen wheelers — that's how they buy products. They don't meet you by the rotisserie chicken and hand you fifty bucks for a dozen books. (The glad news is that this DOES happen in many small book stores and gift shops.)

The three things a big-time book buyer wants to know — if you're lucky enough to get a few minutes with one, and you've piqued their interest — are **(read these carefully ===>)**:

1. Whether your paperbacks are available through the standard on-line wholesalers — usually Ingram (and previously Baker and Taylor).

2. Whether you offer the 'wholesale discount' — 40% off for the store, meaning 55% off for you since you also have to pay 15% to Ingram for the distribution.

3. Whether your books are 'returnable.' 'Returnable' means, tragically for you, that if this store doesn't sell some or all of the books they order, the store gets a *full* refund for each unsold book, regard-

less of the condition in which said books might be returned.

Who pays that refund? LOL, take a wild guess. Yup, these *sold* books are now being returned, and your minuscule royalty, after the 55% discount, is yanked back and deducted from your pathetic monthly check from Ingram Spark (or whatever wholesaler printed and shipped the books to that store). Not only are the books returnable, but they're returnable for a long time! So this reneging can happen well after the sale.

On top of that, it's also you who decides the fate of these returned books.

"Fate?" Dun-de-dun-dun….

You were forced to make the books 'returnable' so they'd qualify for purchase by big book stores. This means returnable to Ingram or whoever shipped them, so that's where they're sent back to. But they're technically yours now because you just bought them back by paying the refund (to this mammoth defaulting store who risked not one dime in carrying your books or anyone else's). Thus, you have to make a choice: Do you want the returned books 'destroyed' (by Ingram, though they actually 'recycle' them, probably into a freebie bin in their employees' break room), or do you want them now shipped to you? LOL, guess who pays the shipping, but at least you get the books, hardly in mint condition.

Nice choices? You like this chapter? I warned you....

It's comical. It's like some horrible board game where you can't believe how badly you're losing. You better read that above paragraph again; it's key info no one will ever tell you, another minor omission by bloggers that prompted me to pen this survival manual to the unsuspecting self-pub masses. We really deserve to understand, in advance, why it's close to impossible to sell to book stores other than small local ones.

But wait, it actually gets worse.... I'm not done. And don't shoot the messenger!

The real heartbreak is this **(again, read carefully ===>)**: in order to have your book on the shelves of *any* decent-sized book store generating real business—books they've ordered through official channels like Ingram at the 55% discount (and 'returnable')—you have to offer that same 55% discount to ALL wholesalers. You can't just target that one individual store or even just all brick and mortar stores, uh-uh, your new discount will apply to **everybody**. So, instead of the 30% minimum discount you're already forced to offer on-line booksellers so that Ingram gets its cut, now you have to offer the 55% discount to every single retailer—this means to every **on-line** bookseller, too. And that includes **Amazon**. As in, all your on-line sales.

I'm kidding, right?

Nope, I'm not. (I'm really, really sorry.)

To repeat, just because silly you wants your books to be available for purchase by regular book stores—and this doesn't suppose they *will* buy your books, just that your books are *available* to them at the wholesale price they absolutely require—you have to extend that same wholesale discount to ALL on-line stores, including Amazon, Barnes and Noble, Kobo, and everyone! ALL your on-line profit will now shrink. Instead of Amazon getting your books at the 30% discount you'd originally set up (30% is the lowest you can offer), the Zon will now get the 55% discount, and you get 25% less for each and every sale. Just to make your books available to book stores, your ENTIRE income from books gets slashed and will remain so as long as you continue offering the 55% discount that brick and mortar stores demand. Even if you're just in *one* bigger, established store. And you thought it might be fitting to have your 'books' in a 'book' store? What's wrong with you?

Still with me? Or are you in a crumpled heap beside the tub, letting the cool tiles sooth your enfeebled sobs?

This is one of the sadder pieces of our reality. You basically have to decide here and now—definitely before you approach major book stores—

whether you want to be in book stores and make nothing across the boards or if you'll forego mainstream book stores altogether but hopefully make more per book selling solely on line, privately, and at smaller stores in your own locale.

I know….

I'm not sure there's anything more depressing for an author than to find out that being in book stores will actually cost you a lot of money, unless you're being sponsored by your husband or wife, mom, dad, or anonymous benefactor, or you've set up your authoring as a non-profit. And, again, no one explains this. They must know it, but they don't want you to, because it's too sickening and they don't want to snuff your flame. They want you to GO FOR IT and to let them help you for a tidy sum.

I mean, it doesn't take more than a day or two of wandering around a strange Colorado town in winter for it to sink in, like snow on the Rockies, that at a $2 profit per book, selling 40 books in a book store over the course of, say, two years, will bring in a whopping $80. You can't even read that sentence with a straight face. Meanwhile, you're simultaneously sacrificing half the booty from your on-line sales for the 'privilege' of being in those stores. Who would do that?!

So no one does. They shuffle back to their desks and bash their heads against on-line retail sites, trying to unravel Amazon algorithms, get more reviews, and somehow make it up the ranks that way. They advertise on FaceBook or Amazon or BookBub. They try to figure out the library possibilities. And this is where the blog hosts know they've got you…. Because if you skip the book store option, expecting to get more through Amazon by bringing your discount back down to 30%, you need to learn every possible trick for getting noticed on Amazon.

How does one get over that depression?

Here's what I did…not advised, just how it panned out for me…. I moseyed into the Barnes & Noble while in Boulder. And there I encountered a surprisingly amenable store manager. She was actually open to me returning in the autumn and doing a book-signing there, but only under the conditions that a) I cleared it with B & N corporate in NYC, and b) I made all three of my current books ('Expedition Costa Rica' would be out by then) available at the 55% wholesale discount at least one month before my book-signing. Another criterion, that plunges author profit to practically zip, is that B & N orders the books for a signing in advance, meaning I'd only get that $2 per book even though I'd be hand-selling them myself at their store.

So I'd fly back to Colorado in September, rent a car, rent lodging, just to spend a Saturday signing books for $2 per book. Say I signed twenty and I made $40 (three months later, when I'd be paid), yippee, that meant I spent about $500 to make $40.

Well, I don't know about you, but doing a book-signing at Barnes & Noble wasn't even on my goal list for that year; I hadn't considered it an option. And when it popped up, I wanted to do it despite sacrifice. Thanks to my day job, and frequently flying right over Colorado anyway, I could spend a few beans on a decent opportunity. So I bowed at the B & N altar and set everything up per their requirements.

I'm inclined to believe that any author would choose a book-signing at B & N over tolerable monetary loss, but I could be wrong. My reasoning was that it was worth a shot to maybe somehow get my books into that store, if perhaps they'd keep a few after the signing. Then, from there, maybe I could work the B & N circuit. I'd never make any money, of course (40 book sales in two years = $80), but to be on book store shelves might be worthwhile in some capacity I'm not yet fully aware of. Though, as I've said, 'exposure' is generally double-speak for 'you pay to have your book somewhere.'

Meanwhile, I'd be taking losses on line from that point. But my sales weren't off the charts anyway, and I could change the discount back to 30% if the book store thing didn't pan out. Nothing like first-hand experimentation. My thinking was, "If I'm *never* going to be in book stores, that's such a tear-jerker that it's worth a try and even a nominal cash outlay to see if the B & N book-signing could have residual advantage." Plus it was another trip to the Rockies.

What kept me from being derailed about the book store bummer was being in for the long haul. I'd either branch into additional book stores after B & N or go back to only selling on line and in small local stores, and getting more per book. Still, it's tragic we can't do both, disgusting the system feels rigged against authors (even though it's really not—everyone just needs their cut), and disturbing that our 'gurus' prefer we don't know.

But, another fact that newbies wouldn't surmise is that self-publishers are a mega market; innocent dream-driven multitudes knowing little-to-nothing about the venture they're embarking upon.

XXXXXXX

- 17 -

"COME BACK NEXT MONDAY"

I know it's been a rough ride through these pages. That is, if you're still aboard this choo-choo. But I love your tenacity and drive. I swear, that's what it takes. And I purposefully made this book inexpensive so no one would just read to the end to get their money's worth. YOU are still reading because you really want the dirt on self-publishing. And I know I haven't gone into the infinite details of every individual task of constructing a nice-looking, nice-reading book all by your lonesome, but only because, as I've said many times, it's all available elsewhere.

I wanted to concentrate on the practical and emotional sides, by unveiling the mythology, ruses, ploys, and businesses built on aspirations of would-be authors. Like you, I walked in knowing squat about publishing. And I now have books out, a couple more on deck, and not only have I not given up, but I intend to duke it out a good while longer.

Believe me, I've given this deep and sober thought, and still don't believe there's a better way for 'regular writers' to publish their books. If I was willing to part with wads of greenbacks, I'd enlist outside talent to reduce my PR responsibility and God knows what else. But the fact is, I've come so far with this, it makes more sense to use my new skills. The learning curve does actually *curve* somewhere around one's third book. (Plus I've taken a fancy to the publishing side.) Why jump ship when I've learned to sail? Might as well continue across the shiny, blue sea.

But...this last bit is hard to even WRITE. Are you sitting down? Maybe pour yourself something stronger than a banana smoothie before tucking into this chapter. It was added to the manuscript a couple of years later, because I scored a few more degrees in the Literary School of Hard Knocks that I felt obliged to share.

Okay, so you're sitting down, you're swilling Malibu Rum and Red Bull with a dash of dashed hopes, and the only reason you're still reading is because there's a sinkful of dinner dishes to deal with the minute you get up from that chair.... Or you're too fat to get up.

You might recall, from the previous chapter, 'Be Yourself and Have Fun,' that I decided to jolly up the marketing process and do things my own way. Since the open road is always beckoning, I devised a sales strategy wherein I'd explore new places while selling books and scheduling future book-signings.

Though I live in Hawai'i, I also keep a car on the Mainland. So I would combine a long road trip with stops at book stores to sell books and to ask about author talks or book-signing opportunities for later in the year. Isn't that what authors do?

That's what authors do.

Yeah, some authors. Famous authors. Authors with publishing houses pre-arranging their tours. Or those with solvent, supportive spouses.

For personal, practical, financial, and logistical reasons, I chose Northern California. It was January 2018, I'd just released my fourth book, 'Stars in Our Eyes,' a collection of true stories, and was high on the fumes of that. I had about forty reviews on Amazon for all my books and all but two were five stars, so I felt pretty legit at that point.

I prefer live contact, too, and have always found it more effective. An email query can be brushed off with a click, but it's harder to shine on a red-blooded writer flashing their masterpiece and a toothy grin. If you were holding an event, would you sign up someone you've never met in lieu of a charming (fetchingly plump and bleary-eyed) live specimen in front of you?

So, I lined up one really nice event in Grass Valley, up near the Nevada border in northeastern California. This book store had a big regional writers group that met there once a month and the store always provided an author speaker. The store owners were delightful, dug me and my books, and said I could be their guest speaker for either September or October, my choice. They only took books on consignment, but at the event, authors got 100% of the proceeds from book sales. An excellent deal.

I said I'd phone them soon with my selected date, and left them eight books (two of each of my titles) on consignment. I'd pick up my check for the books when I returned for the autumn talk. Then I resumed my journey. I was only a few days on the road and I had already sold a bunch of books to a writers group in Sebastopol, one to my hostess at the Air B & B in Grass Valley, and now eight on consignment, plus a nifty event scheduled—things were cookin'.

I have to say that, regardless of any credentials or status, cold calling is never easy. Any confidence you might rightfully be entitled to deserts you when you march into a strange book store in a strange town, books in hand. No matter how convincingly your angels insist that book stores love books, love authors, and will love you, you're still just a traveling salesman, "Ma'am, I'd like to show you this new model (of vacuum cleaner)." As you approach the counter in search of the store's owner or buyer, you feel your worst demons tugging your coattails, trying to drag you back out of the store.

But you hoist that courageous smile. You didn't just drive 150 miles for nothing. Besides, there's no reason to feel phony or out of place — you're exactly where you're supposed to be, in a BOOK STORE with your BOOKS. For the love of Haagen-Dazs, if it weren't for us, there would be no book stores!

But let me backtrack one second before continuing with this cliff-hanger….

How do you prepare for a book-selling safari by car? You need books, right? How many? Guess what, that's an unknown quantity; there's no guess-timate how many books you'll need or which of your titles will sell the most. But you don't want to run short, because there's no way to rapidly acquire more. (Unless Mom is standing by to ship some and willing to pay the UPS bill, while you wait in some Motel Six for the shipment.) So you play it safe and haul with you extra boxes of all your titles. (Same as when you go to a book-signing, you over-prepare so as not to run out. You might only sell two, but you might sell dozens.) This, however, means ordering the books in advance so they're at arm's length on your trip. Sorry, more money forked out for books that might well become closet inventory in the likely event they're unsold.

Okay, back to the selling crusade. The good news on a road cruise is:

1. It's surprisingly easy to find the one or two book stores in a medium-sized town — just ask anyone, or simply look for it on Main Street.

2. Yes, book stores thrive on books and you've got some in your mittens, so you're not unwelcome.

3. Book store owners and workers are, by and large, polite and educated. Plus, they're generally curious and are avid readers. Also, you could be a potential customer, so courtesy rules.

4. They can't survive without authors, so pandering to our lot is part of their job description.

5. I had my four books, a sleek one-sheet containing all my info, and a cheerful disposition.

6. Many book stores really do schedule author events monthly or even weekly. And they usually also have some policy about either local-author

books or self-published books. (Usually you'll pay to be on their shelves.)

Now the bad news about cold calling in a region you don't live in:

1. Being either local, having a brand new book, or having a book with a catchy hook are what they're looking for.

2. They will just about never buy books directly from you. Self-published books are primarily taken on consignment. So you have to donate books and somehow get paid later…yeah, right. Or they might say they'll order your books from your distributor, "Just leave us your info." Yeah, right.

3. You've just spent a lot of money on gas to get to this town, not to mention your motels.

Now for the really bad news, that at first seems like good news:

1. If the owner/buyer is in the store when you boogie in, you can learn about their author events. But if said individual isn't in, you have to come back when s/he is. You must decide if it's worth waiting (usually at least a day or two) to meet this person, who does all the scheduling.

2. Stores that offer book-signings or author talks have set dates for these—like the first Thursday night of the month or every Saturday afternoon or every second Friday evening, etc. And authors are normally booked well in advance.

3. At events, each store has different terms for how much profit you can make per book sold and how much they'll take, but you'll be supplying the books—so the hauling and shipping are on you. (Feel a Hemingway coming on?)

4. Let's say Ms. Riley, the store owner, is in house when you parachute in and says she'll sign you on for an event. "Great!" you emote. "When?" (It's now January.)

She says there's an opening April 8, or you can have any Thursday night after August.

"Great!" you repeat. "I'll think about which date and give you a call!"

What's wrong here? It's just what you wanted!

Think about it—you're making this big loop from city to city, store to store. You're being well received, once you grow accustomed to feeling like a hand-grenade hurled into the store by a terrorist. And the stores are even offering you appearances. But how do you show up in Grass Valley, California on October 12 for an awesome talk totally worth doing, then also get to Eureka, California for a Sunday in April, then to Ashland, Oregon a week after that? Where do you spend those days or months in between? Or if you somehow manage to schedule appearances back-to-back, how do you get from one city to the other fast enough by car, or cheap enough by plane (with all those book boxes and then renting a car)?

This became the puzzle of my outing. I got all kinds of leads and future offers. The further down the calendar I was willing to appear, the easier it was to get booked. But could I arrange the dates in a viable sequence? I'd want to do my whole tour in about ten days or two weeks, wouldn't I? Yet most of the events are on the weekends.… Hmm.

And, sadly, appearances really *are* about exposure more than income. To expect to sell 20 books in some quaint West Coast book shop is optimistic. You might sell 10, or even less. And you're sharing the proceeds with the book store—not the net balance, but the gross balance. Shipping and printing costs aren't factored in, you're divvying up the retail price paid per book—maybe 60% for you and 40% for the store (it varies). So, you'll maybe take away just a few bucks per book. Think about it.

You meet nice folks, you acquire new email addresses, you may lay the groundwork for a return next year if you're so inclined, but is it worth the time and travel? Only if you do sequential events with well-orchestrated dates, at stores within a few hours of each other.

Again, if you're lavishly sponsored, then zoom around by air, pay baggage fees for all the book boxes, rent cars, and stay in motels. Mom or that secret admirer can spring for the $300-500 per stop, plus the cost of stocking up on books you may or may not need. But all for a few email addresses per stop and 2 to 20 book sales for almost nothing per book? Oh, and maybe you can also leave a few of each title with the stores on consignment and chase up the money later. Good luck widdat.

So, even with your sugar daddy, it's rocket science scheduling events that allow you to move from one venue to the next in a timely manner. There will be weeks or months between appearances; or at best you'll set up two in the same week but not in the same town. Logistical nightmare. Unless camping and hiking are your passions, then you can work the surrounding mountain ranges in your down time.

And don't forget, you'll have heavy boxes in tow. Not only is each box an extra $25 on the plane, but you must get them all to and from the airport, to and from the check-in counter, and from baggage claim to the rental car place. If you happen to be crunching numbers while you're also gritting your teeth, you'll probably ask yourself if this is fun.

It could be, if you have a huge ego, the luxury of time, and a fat wallet. You can tell everyone you're on an author tour, selling books, and scheduling talks. You can pump yourself up like you're livin' the dream. See yourself as Ernie Hemingway when he wrote 'Death in the Afternoon' in sunny Spain. And you can scribe the next great American novel in a string of Starbucks' in between illustrious speaking engagements up and down the state.

As for me, touching into book stores terribly far apart, I began to sense the foolery in returning later in the year for modest appearances hither and yon. Best-case scenarios of selling two dozen books would cost way more than I'd make, not to mention time away from home and other responsibilities. And did I really want to repeat this identical trip on my next getaway? Returning to these same towns had much less appeal than sightseeing the first time through.
Sad.

"Well, why hit the real highway when you can cruise the information highway without budging or paying a dime?" you will surely ask.
Because hunched-over, nature-deprived writers, chained to their desks and keyboards, are dying for oxygen and open meadows. Sure, you can email every book store and library in the nation; you'll get

responses, probably even nibbles. They may ask for more info about you and your books. But the person replying to your queries is paid by the hour to answer emails, nothing's at stake on their end. Not so in your case, where everything's at stake! Knocking out query upon query, though it may seem productive, still leaves you yoked to your computer. Simultaneously, you have to keep records of all your correspondence, in case Marian the Librarian actually responds, you'll know who she is. A ton of effort.

Or perhaps, through querying, you've managed to land a book-signing at a store in Seattle or New Orleans. Peachy, what do you do with that? Fly or drive to Washington or Louisiana for a three-hour meet-and-greet next June?

You see where all this is going? In a big circle leading straight back to square one.

Sad.

I ended up not following up on any of the author events I learned about, and foregoing the one I agreed to in Grass Valley. I'm gonna fly all the way there from Hawai'i for one author talk? Ship enough books so I have a bunch to sell, then ship the leftovers back to Hawai'i? I never even called to see if my eight books sold; since I dropped the ball on the event, I didn't want to chase after the diddly book sale money. But, once reality banged me over the head, I simply couldn't justify going all the way back there....

Too bad I didn't have a survival manual alerting me to obstacles I'd encounter. Sure, I had an adventure I don't regret, but I can only shrug regarding taking one's show on the road. Maybe better to pack up a table and hit book fairs in some sequence…. There, again, you've got to either transport enough books with you or have somewhere to pick them up near your destinations. It's beyond tricky, might be good for wealthy retirees, and is probably best-suited for flush ego-trippers who find glamour in 'being an author.' (Less glamorous by the year.) Possibly there's some other angle to it I haven't considered. I'm open to suggestion. Let me know if you come up with anything. And, of course, the subject matter of your books weighs mightily into where you'd go, why, and what success you can have out there.

I will add here, with a sincere thumbs up, that I think a self-pubbed author's best bet for on-the-ground selling and for ACTUAL exposure and visibility, is to work one or two expansive metropolitan areas. Preferably a great city or two within a couple of hours of your home or the home of loved ones you like to visit. Cities where your day job frequently sends you could also be appropriate, if you have spare time on work trips. At the very least, huge urban centers not too far away where you can enjoy leisure time as well as selling books.

I know, this (?) from an author who resides in the Sandwich Islands? (Literally the most remote archipelago on the planet.)

But by casting your net over a large metropolis or two, you can become regionally established. You'll have that preferred 'local' status, you'll build relationships with book and gift shops that get to know you, and you can easily keep track of books you choose to leave on consignment. In the city libraries, you can become known, and friends can stop in and request your books. And you can schedule author appearances and re-appearances throughout the community with the confidence that you're able to show up.

This 'big city' aha comes to me as a sort of conclusion after writing this book. Reviewing my ad hoc episodes out riding the range, it makes way more sense to focus on one large area close to one's home. But, of course, you may be geographically challenged like me, so it won't work for everyone.

XOXOXOX

- 18 -

TAKE STOCK OF HOW FAR YOU'VE COME

What makes someone want to write a book?
There's something about you or your story
that you're compelled to share. Perhaps you have a
quirky turn-of-phrase, an exotic imagination, and/
or a flair for description. Maybe you have interesting, bizarre, shocking, or enlightening factoids you
think people should know about. Maybe you're
outstanding in your field — you've discovered a
new planet, you're a culinary marvel, or a dating
disaster. The drive to self-publish springs from zest,
fun, fire, motivation. Play to your strength. Don't
be afraid to be zany or analytical or political or dot-
dot-dot. Whatever floats your boat will also float
your book. If you're clear on what it is that keeps
you excited, you'll be okay.

No two people have the same skills or visions, so the more YOU you are, the stronger your material will be. One of the beautiful things about books is that readers appreciate a unique slant, expertise, strange and imaginative tales. Books are magical. And good writing is a magic wand.

So stay in your zone. Don't be afraid of yourself. And don't shy away from major overtime, ruthless edits, and re-writes — it all ups the worth of the work.

Enjoy your process. Keep creating, and murdering darlings (when in doubt, throw it out). In the end, if there is an end to this, we'll have our beautiful books forever, to share with whomever. Make them strong, make them fine, make them attractive. And if one day you're no longer writing, if you're on to something else, you've left a wonderful and enduring legacy.

Being an author is a world of illusion, in some ways as far out there as the stories we transfer from the ethers onto the page. But it's a rich destiny that can keep your wheels turning for years or decades. If you're in need of big thumps on the back, though, or six-figure income, floods of five-star reviews, and new readers lining up, you better take a deep breath and climb into your marketing suit on steroids.

One of the most valuable exercises we can do is to look back to where our business was a year ago. Looking at our previous goals, we observe how we've grown, changed, and advanced. Nothing ever goes exactly as expected, self-publishing no exception. Most accomplishments seem far more exciting as distant dreams than when we're grinding out the reality. Ask any parent. Any basking in the golden rays of glory is fleeting, maybe a moment here or there when you pinch yourself in acknowledgement that what was once a hazy mirage is now your day-to-day life. But at that same moment, you're no doubt intently reaching for the next hazy mirage.

The author odyssey unfolds. Though there's no one big moment where your ship comes in, you still did it, and hallelujah!

XOX

I don't know where this trail will take me, but I do know I now have lovely books that I thumb through periodically and that bring a smile to my face. Sitting in my armchair in a sunny window, reading a book, it's almost impossible to believe that I wrote it, I designed it, I formatted it, and I published it. And…people everywhere have read or are reading it. And I'll continue adding books to my self-shelf.

Even though no one in the on-line self-publishing community tells us the gnarly stuff, so as not to burst bubbles, I still thank them all. As you make your way through the dark DIY night, their abundant sharing will absolutely light the path. Every resource you'll need is at your fingertips.

I started out green with a dream; the trip hasn't been anything like I expected; but there's no way I'm turning back. I'm just getting started. Stacks of white pages once in file boxes are now bound books on my shelf and all over the worldwide web; they're in libraries, in stores, and on other people's bookshelves. Not bad for starters.

It's hard to wrap this book up, because there's always more, and always will be in the world of writing and publishing books. Through this previously unheard of opportunity, today we can take the reins into our own hands. And one day soon, we'll almost certainly look back to see that authors of this era were on the crest of something that changed books and publishing forever. Self-publishing is a definite dawn.

XOXOXOX

- END -

Good, you survived this book! A lot to digest. Now off to publish your own!

If you're curious about my other books, they're listed on the following page. And at Amazon.com, of course, where you can read the reviews. And add new ones.

My website is WendyRaebeck.com, where I post updates. I also send newsy emails to my list. Please sign on via the CONTACTS page of my website, where your comments are always welcome.

Glad you stayed. I wish you strength, the joy of writing, clever ideas, and wonderful books with your name on them.

Blessings and aloha,
Shamelessly,

~ Ava, a.k.a. Wendy

OTHER BOOKS BY

W. M. RAEBECK
(a.k.a. Ava Greene)

I DID INHALE -- MEMOIR OF
A HIPPIE CHICK

SOME SWAMIS ARE FAT

EXPEDITION COSTA RICA

STARS IN OUR EYES - true stories

NICARAGUA STORY - BACK
ROADS OF THE CONTRA WAR

SILENCE OF ISLANDS - poems

TA TA FOR NOW - the Movie

- all available in print and ebook -
- (audio coming soon) -

Visit WendyRaebeck.com
for more info